Signing

BLACKLINE MASTERS

SHARE

the

Music

MACMILLAN
McGRAW-HILL

SERIES AUTHORS

Judy Bond
Coordinating Author

René Boyer-White

Margaret Campbelle-duGard

Marilyn Copeland Davidson
Coordinating Author

Robert de Frece

Mary Goetze
Coordinating Author

Doug Goodkin

Betsy M. Henderson

Michael Jothen

Carol King

Vincent P. Lawrence
Coordinating Author

Nancy L. T. Miller

Ivy Rawlins

Susan Snyder
Coordinating Author

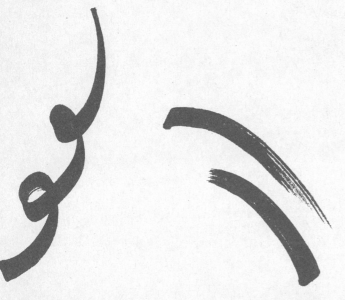

Macmillan/McGraw-Hill School Publishing Company

New York • Columbus

Teri Burdette, the writer of the two *Signing* books for *Share the Music*, is a music teacher at Lucy Barnsley Elementary School in Rockville, Maryland. Since 1980 she has taught deaf, hearing impaired, and hearing students in a mainstreamed program. Teri formed the Flying Fingers, a group of performing fifth graders, to help raise the awareness that "Music and Sign Language Are for Everyone!"

Macmillan/McGraw-Hill School Division
10 Union Square East
New York, New York 10003

Printed in the United States of America

ISBN 0-02-295102-4 / K–2

4 5 6 7 8 9 DBH 99 98 97 96

INTRODUCTION

In the music classroom, sign language becomes more than a mode of communication. It offers yet another unique vehicle for learning and musical expression. Sign language can enhance the performance of a song and, as in choral choreography, add interest for the participant as well as the observer.

The use of sign language in songs is conceptual, not literal. The objective is to paint a picture, and it is therefore not necessary to sign every word, although all words are sung. Articles and many pronouns are eliminated in sign. Also, since a word may have more than one meaning, it may have more than one sign.

In conversation many words do not have specific signs and are fingerspelled using the manual alphabet. Fingerspelling is so small it is usually avoided in songs. However, since many signs are based on the manual alphabet, it is included at the back of the book as a reference guide. If a particular phrase or idea does not lend itself to sign, a combination sign, gesture, and mime is used. Examples of this are indicated by the use of the word *Gesture* at the beginning of the signing directions in this book.

Sign language does not rely solely on the use of hands. Facial expressions and body movements are very important; this is how the mood of the song is conveyed to the audience.

Signs should flow from one to the next, keeping in mind the rhythm of the song, and should match the length of the phrases. The signing of songs should also include very large movements so that the audience can see them.

The illustrations and signing instructions in this book are directed to a right-handed student. Students who are left-handed should reverse the hands. However, for beginning sign-language work, don't worry about right and left. If students ask which hand to use, respond by saying, "The hand that you write with is the one that does the most moving."

When students perform, put the left-handed signers on the ends of the rows to avoid collision with fellow students. For best visual results, have students wear colors contrasting to skin color so that the hands are highlighted. Solid shirts are a must since prints and geometrics confuse the eye.

There are many different ways to sign the same phrase or thought. The sign language in this book is *one* approach to learning songs in sign. Also, sign language is colloquial and can vary in different parts of the country.

Students should start with vocabulary that is meaningful. It is fine to sign just a few appropriate words or to use a sign ostinato. Using a "how to" verbiage while showing students a sign can help those who learn by hearing, as watching can help those who learn better by seeing. Don't worry about perfection. The emphasis should be on enjoyment and fun! The signers' hands will become better able to find the positions with each new experience.

—Teri Burdette

TABLE OF CONTENTS

KINDERGARTEN

KINDERGARTEN

Name

1. uno (one)

2. dos (two)

Add the signs for the numbers in the song. Notice that you can count using only one hand in sign language.

3. tres (three)

4. cuatro (four)

Macmillan/McGraw-Hill

Counting Song (Page 2)

5. cinco (five)

6. seis (six)

7. siete (seven)

8. ocho (eight)

Macmillan/McGraw-Hill

Counting Song (Page 3)

9. nueve (nine)

10. diez (ten)

Macmillan/McGraw-Hill

Twinkle, Twinkle, Little Star (Page 1)

1. twinkle

With your hands held high, flip your middle fingers outward off your thumbs using alternate hands.

2. star

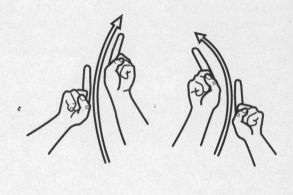

Hit the sides of your upright index fingers against each other as you move them upward.

3. how

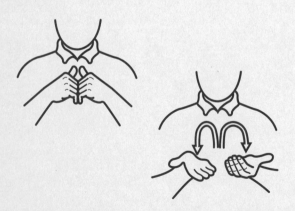

With palms down, curve your fingers and touch the fingernails of both hands together. Then turn the hands to palms up.

4. wonder

Make a circle at your forehead with your right index finger.

Twinkle, Twinkle, Little Star (Page 2)

5. what

Point your right index finger, and move it down across the fingers of your left hand, close to the palm.

6. you

Point your right index finger to the stars.

7. are

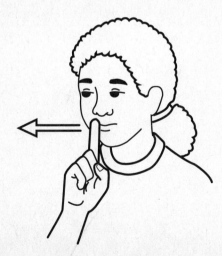

Touch your lips with the tip of your right index finger. Then move the hand straight ahead.

8. up above the world so high

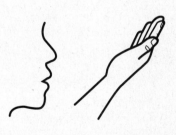

Gesture upward with your open right hand, palm facing in.

Macmillan/McGraw-Hill

Twinkle, Twinkle, Little Star (Page 3)

9. like

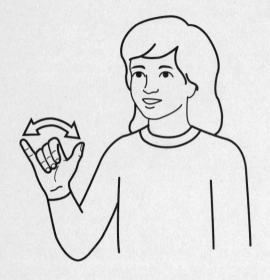

Hold your right hand in the "Y" position, with palm facing out, and move the hand from side to side.

10. diamond (shining)

Move your middle fingers up and apart while wiggling them.

11. sky

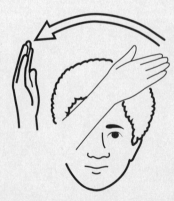

Make a large arc above your head with your right hand.

Bell Horses (Page 1)

1. bell

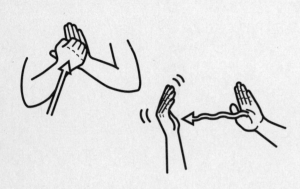

Hit the open palm of your left hand with your right fist. Then move your right hand out, opening and shaking it as it moves.

2. horses

Hold your right hand in the "H" position, touch the thumb to your temple, and move the index and middle fingers up and down. (You can use both hands for this sign.)

3. what's (what)

Point your right index finger, and move it down across the fingers of your left hand, close to the palm.

4. time

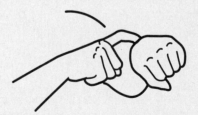

Point to the back of your left wrist with your right index finger.

Macmillan/McGraw-Hill

SIGNING MASTER S•K•3

Bell Horses (Page 2)

5. day

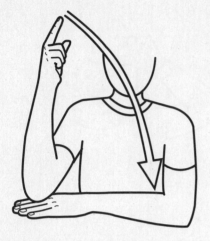

Hold your left palm down. Rest your right elbow on your left hand, and point your right index finger up. Then move your right hand in an arc to your left elbow.

6. one

Hold up your right index finger.

7. two

Hold up the index finger and middle finger of your right hand.

8. to away (leave)

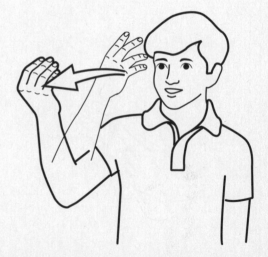

Hold your open right hand, palm in, near your face. Then move the hand forward and away from the face while closing the fingers.

Kindergarten • Use with page T82.

Star Light, Star Bright (Page 1)

1. star

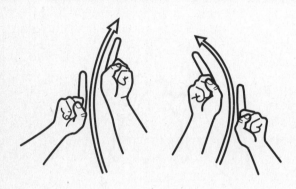

Hit the sides of your upright index fingers against each other as you move them upward.

2. light

With your hands held high, flip your middle fingers outward off your thumbs using alternate hands.

3. bright

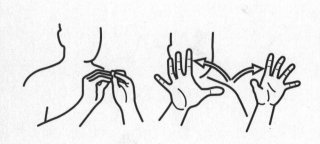

Hold both hands with palms out and fingers touching. Then move them up and to the sides, opening them to the "5" position.

4. tonight (now night)

Hold both hands in the "Y" position, palms up, and drop them down. Then rest the right hand, in a bent position, on top of the left, which is held palm down.

Macmillan/McGraw-Hill

Star Light, Star Bright (Page 2)

5. wish

Touch your chest with your right hand, in the "C" position, with palm in. Then move the hand down.

6. may

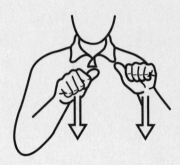

Hold both of your hands in the "A" position, with palms down, and move them down together.

7. might (maybe)

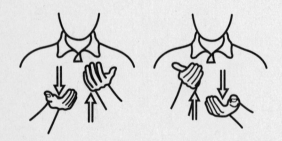

With both of your palms up, move your hands alternately up and down, as in weighing something.

8. have

Touch your chest with the fingertips of your bent hands.

The Bear Went Over the Mountain (Page 1)

I. bear

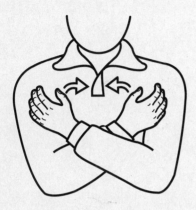

Cross your arms at your chest, with palms in and fingertips curved. Then move your hands toward the center of your body.

2. over

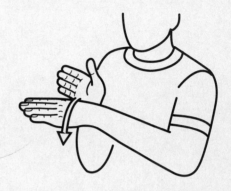

Hold your left hand parallel to the ground, palm down. Touch the little-finger side of your right hand to the top of the left hand, and move it across the hand.

3. mountain

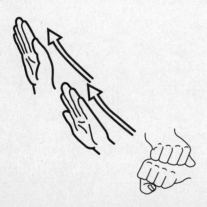

Strike your fists together, palms down and right fist above the left. Then raise your open hands toward your right side.

4. see

Touch your right hand, in the "V" position, to beneath your right eye. Then move the hand forward.

Macmillan/McGraw-Hill

5. could

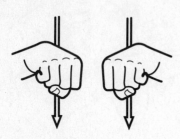

Move both of your fists downward in front of your chest.

6. all

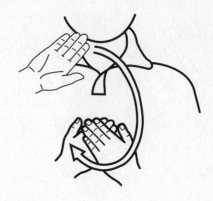

Make a circle with your right hand around your left hand, ending with the right hand in the palm of the left, with palms up.

7. other

Hold your right hand in the "A" position, with palm down. Then move the thumb to the right as you turn the palm up.

8. side

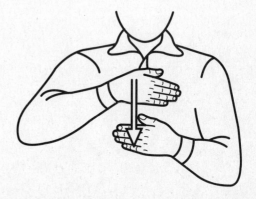

Hold both palms facing in, with the right hand above the left hand. Then move the right hand down parallel to the left.

Macmillan/McGraw-Hill

Name _____

Three Little Fishies (Page 1)

1. three

Hold up the thumb, index finger, and middle finger of your right hand.

2. fishies (fish)

Touch the inside of your right wrist with your left hand, and move your right hand, with thumb up, back and forth.

3. mama

With your right hand in the "5" position, touch the thumb to your chin.

4. swim/swam

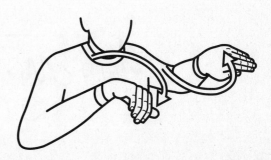

Use both of your hands to imitate swimming the breaststroke.

Three Little Fishies (Page 2)

5. over

Hold your left hand parallel to the ground, palm down. Touch the little-finger side of your right hand to the top of the left hand, and move it across the hand.

6. dam

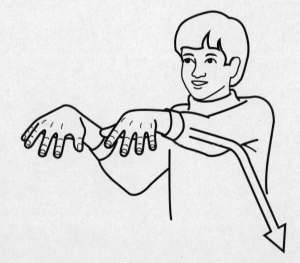

(Gesture) Move both hands from in front of your right shoulder, down and to the left, imitating water running over a dam.

I. jingle bells

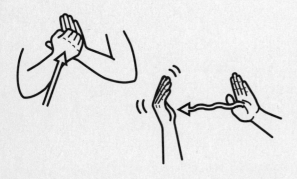

Hit the open palm of your left hand with your right fist. Then move your right hand out, opening and shaking it as it moves.

2. all

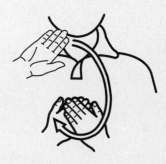

Make a circle with your right hand around your left hand, ending with the right hand in the palm of the left, with palms up.

3. way

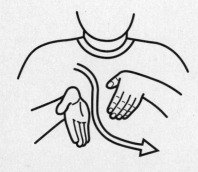

Hold your open hands facing each other, fingers pointing forward and thumbs up, and move them forward in a winding manner.

4. what

Point your right index finger, and move it down across the fingers of your left hand, close to the palm.

Jingle Bells (Page 2)

5. fun

Hold both hands in the "H" position. Brush your nose with the tips of the fingers of the right hand. Then move the hand down and brush the fingers of the left hand.

6. is

Touch your lips with the tip of your right index finger. Then move the hand straight ahead.

7. ride

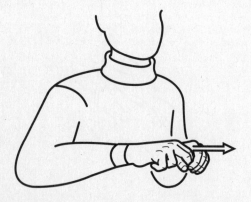

Hold your right hand in a curved "V" position. Hold your left hand in the "O" position. Move the right hand into the left, and move both hands forward.

8. one

Hold up your right index finger.

Name_____

9. horse

Hold your right hand in the "H" position, touch the thumb to your temple, and move the index and middle fingers up and down. (You can use both hands for this sign.)

10. sleigh

Hold both of your hands in a curved "V" position, with palms up. Move the hands back and forth together.

Macmillan/McGraw-Hill

Name_____

1. must

Hold your right hand in the "X" position, and move it down several times.

2. be

Touch your lips with the tip of your right index finger. Then move the hand straight ahead.

3. Santa

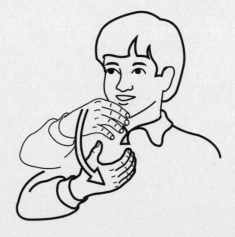

With your right hand in the "C" position, outline a letter C from your chin to your chest.

Macmillan/McGraw-Hill

Big Beautiful Planet (Page 1)

1. there's (is)

Touch your lips with the tip of your right index finger. Then move the hand straight ahead.

2. big

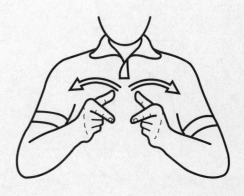

Hold both of your hands in the "L" position, with palms facing each other. Then draw the hands apart.

3. beautiful

Hold your right hand closed, palm in, at your chin. Then open the hand, and circle your face, coming to rest at the chin.

4. planet/earth

Touch the thumb and middle finger of your right hand to the back of your left fist, and move the right hand back and forth.

5. sky

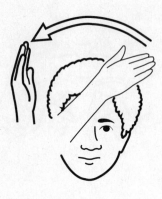

Make a large arc above your head with your right hand.

6. my

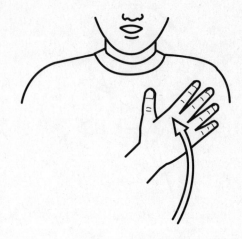

Touch your chest with your open right hand.

7. home

Touch your lips with your closed right hand. Then move the hand to touch your right cheek.

8. where

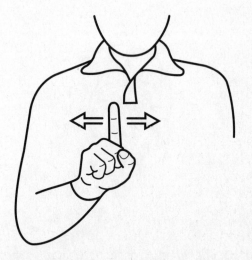

Hold up your right index finger, with the palm of the hand out, and move it back and forth.

Macmillan/McGraw-Hill

Big Beautiful Planet (Page 3)

9. live

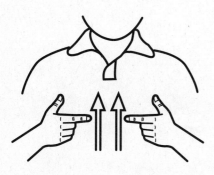

Move both of your hands, in the "L" position, up the middle of your body.

10. you

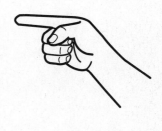

Point your right index finger to the person you are talking to.

11. many

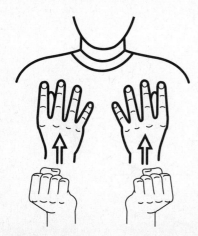

Hold both of your hands in the "S" position, with palms up, and open and close them quickly several times.

12. others

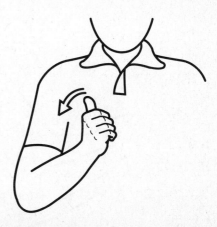

Hold your right hand in the "A" position, with palm down. Then move the thumb to the right as you turn the palm up.

Big Beautiful Planet (Page 4)

13. too

Hold your index fingers side by side, pointing forward. Move them together, apart, and together again.

14. we

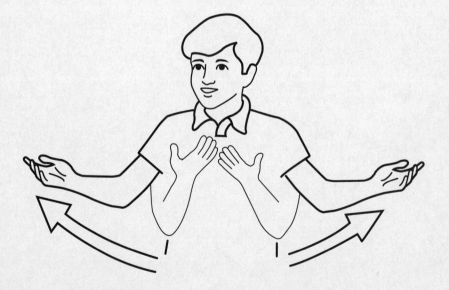

(Gesture) Hold your hands together, with palms up and fingers touching. Then move them apart in a sweeping gesture.

Macmillan/McGraw-Hill

GRADE 1

		TEACHER'S EDITION page	SIGNING MASTER page

GRADE 1

The Old Gray Cat (Page 1)

1. cat

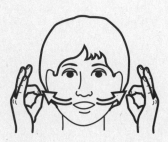

Move your hands, in the "F" position, outward from the sides of your mouth to show whiskers.

2. sleeping

Lay your head on your right hand in the natural gesture of sleeping. Change hands each time the word sleeping *occurs.*

3. house

Using both of your hands, outline the shape of a roof and house.

4. mice

Touch the tip of your nose with the upright index finger of your right hand.

5. creeping

Extend and bend the thumb, index finger, and middle finger of each hand. Move one hand in front of the other in a creeping manner. Use small movements for the mice and big ones for the cat.

6. nibbling (eat)

Touch your mouth with the closed fingertips of your right hand.

7. scamper

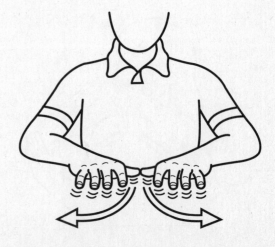

Hold your hands palms down, with all fingers extended and bent. Wiggle the hands away from your body to suggest mice running everywhere.

Name_____

I Know an Old Lady (Page 1)

1. fly

Catch an imaginary fly on your left arm.

2. guess

Move your right hand, in the "C" position, in front of your forehead, and change it to the "S" position.

3. she'll

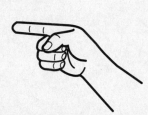

Point your right index finger to the place where the "old lady" is.

4. die

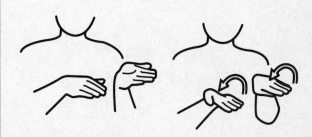

Point the fingers of both hands straight ahead, with the right palm down and the left palm up. Then turn both hands over.

I Know an Old Lady (Page 2)

5. spider

Cross your hands, palms down, and link the little fingers. Then curve and wiggle your other fingers as you move the hands forward.

6. bird

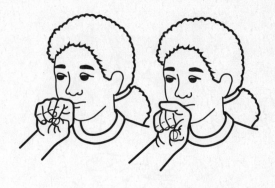

Hold the back of your right hand against your lips, and use your thumb and index finger to show a beak opening and closing.

7. cat

Move your hands, in the "F" position, outward from the sides of your mouth to show whiskers.

8. dog

Pat your leg with your right hand, and snap the fingers.

I Know an Old Lady (Page 3)

9. goat

Hold your right hand, in the "S" position, at your chin to show a beard. Then move the hand to your forehead, in the "V" position, to show horns.

10. cow

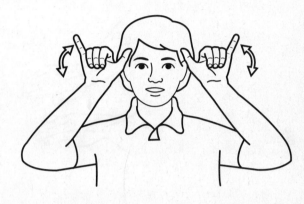

With both of your hands in the "Y" position, hold the thumbs at your forehead, and pivot the hands up and down to show horns.

11. horse

Hold your right hand in the "H" position, touch the thumb to your temple, and move the index and middle fingers up and down. (You can use both hands for this sign.)

Name_____

SIGNING MASTER S•1•3

Stop and Go

I. walk

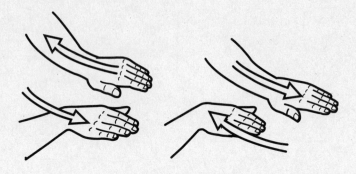

Use your hands, with palms down, to show the movement of feet, one in front of the other.

---

2. stop

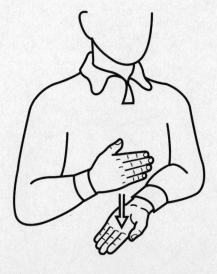

Hold your left hand open, with palm up. Hold your right hand open above it, with palm facing left. Move the right hand down emphatically to a position across the left palm.

30

Grade 1 • Use with page T88.

Macmillan/McGraw-Hill

Name_____

1. weave

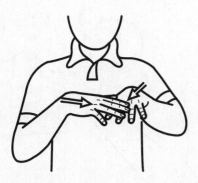

Hold both hands in the "5" position, palms down. Slide the right hand across the left, then the left hand across the right.

2. sunshine

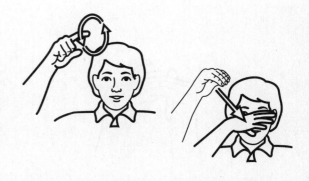

Circle your right index finger above your head. Then close the fingertips, and move the hand down while opening it.

3. out of

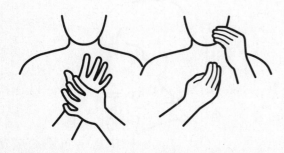

Hold your right hand, palm in, in your left hand. Move the right hand down, out of the left, and close the fingers of both hands.

4. falling rain (rain)

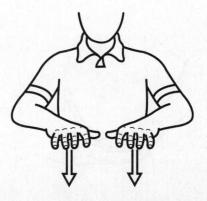

With palms down and fingers curved, move your hands downward in short, quick motions.

Macmillan/McGraw-Hill

Weave Me the Sunshine (Page 2)

5. build

Place the downturned fingertips of each hand repeatedly one on top of the other.

6. hope

Point your right index finger to your forehead. Then, with one hand above your head and palms facing, bend both hands at the same time.

7. new

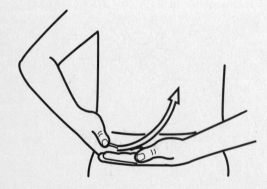

With both hands palms up and fingertips pointing to each other, move your right hand across the palm of your left hand and then up.

8. tomorrow

With your right hand in the "A" position, touch the thumb to your cheek, and then move the hand forward.

32

Macmillan/McGraw-Hill

Weave Me the Sunshine (Page 3)

9. fill

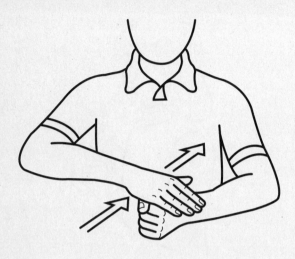

Hold your left hand in the "S" position. Move your open right hand, palm down, across the top of the left toward your body.

10. cup

Hold your left hand open, with palm up. Move your right hand, in the "C" position, upward from the left palm.

11. again

Hold your left hand open, palm up and fingers together. Turn your bent right hand, from palm up, over and into the left palm.

We Are Playing in the Forest (Page 1)

1. we/us

(Gesture) Hold your hands together, with palms up and fingers touching. Then move them apart in a sweeping gesture.

2. playing/play

Hold both of your hands in the "Y" position, and shake them several times.

3. forest

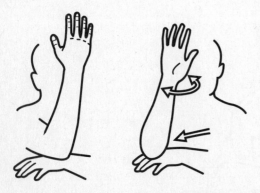

Move the elbow of your upright right arm from the back of your left wrist to the fingertips while turning your open right hand back and forth.

4. for (because)

Touch your forehead with your right index finger. Then move the hand to the right and into the "A" position.

Macmillan/McGraw-Hill

We Are Playing in the Forest (Page 2)

5. wolf

Hold your right hand near your nose, with palm in and fingers open. Then pull the hand out, and close the fingers.

6. far away

Hold both hands in the "A" position, with palms facing and fingers touching. Then move the right hand forward.

7. who

Make a circle in front of your mouth with your right index finger.

8. knows

Touch your forehead with the fingertips of your right hand.

We Are Playing in the Forest (Page 3)

9. what

Point your right index finger, and move it down across the fingers of your left hand, close to the palm.

10. will

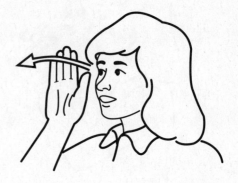

Move your upright right hand, palm facing left, from the side of your face, slightly up and forward.

11. happen

Point both index fingers away from your body, with palms facing. Then turn your hands so the palms are facing down.

12. if

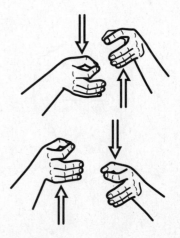

Hold both hands in the "F" position, with palms facing each other. Then move the hands alternately up and down.

Macmillan/McGraw-Hill

We Are Playing in the Forest (Page 4)

13. finds

Bring your open right hand, palm facing out, to your chest while closing the thumb and index finger.

One Light, One Sun (Page 1)

1. one light

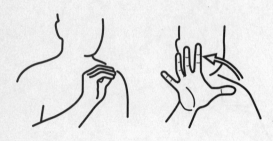

Hold your right hand with palm out and fingers touching on the word *one*. Open the fingers on the word *light*.

2. one

Hold up your right index finger.

3. sun

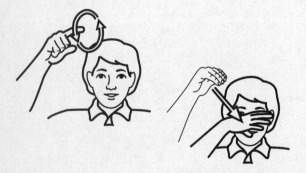

Circle your right index finger above your head. Then close the fingertips, and move the hand down while opening it.

4. lighting

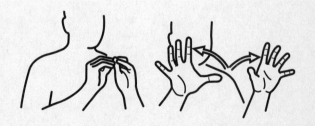

Hold both hands with palms out and fingers touching. Then move them up and to the sides, opening them to the "5" position.

—Macmillan/McGraw-Hill

One Light, One Sun (Page 2)

5. ev'ryone

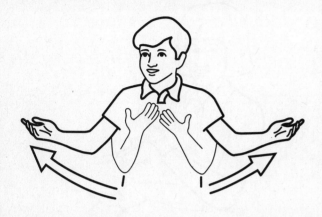

(Gesture) Hold your hands together, with palms up and fingers touching. Then move them apart in a sweeping gesture.

6. world

With both hands in the "W" position, circle the right hand around the left, and rest it on the left index finger.

7. turning

Circle your right index finger, pointed down, around your upright left index finger.

8. home

Touch your lips with your closed right hand. Then move the hand to touch your right cheek.

9. dream

Wiggle your right index finger as you move it away from your forehead.

10. song

Move your right hand back and forth over your left forearm. This shows the movement of the conductor's hand.

11. heard

Hold your right hand, slightly cupped, behind your ear.

12. love

With both of your hands in the "S" position, palms in, cross your wrists over your heart.

Name_____

13. heart

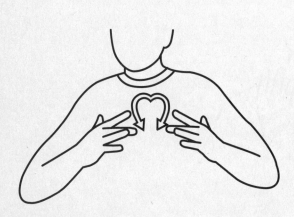

Draw the shape of a heart on your chest with your middle fingers.

14. warming

Begin with your closed right hand, palm in, at your chin. Move the hand upward to your mouth, opening the hand as it moves.

15. hope

Point your right index finger to your forehead. Then, with one hand above your head and palms facing, bend both hands at the same time.

16. joy

Pat your chest with your open hands in an upward motion.

Macmillan/McGraw-Hill

17. **filling (inspiring)**

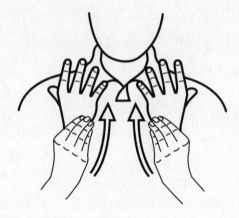

Move your hands, fingers touching, from your waist upward, opening them as they move.

Macmillan/McGraw-Hill

Happy Birthday (Page 1)

1. happy

Pat your chest with your open hands in an upward motion.

2. birthday

Move your right hand from your stomach into the palm of your left hand, with both palms up.

3. to

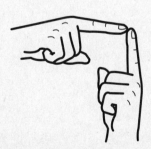

Point the index finger of your right hand to the tip of the upright index finger of your left hand.

4. you

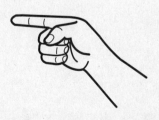

Point your right index finger to the appropriate person.

5. **dear (sweet)**

Move the fingertips of your right hand down across your chin.

Name _____

A Time for Love (Page 1)

1. December (winter)

Hold both hands in the "S" position, with palms facing, and gently shake them, as in shivering from the cold.

2. time

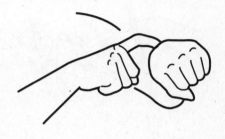

Point to the back of your left wrist with your right index finger.

3. ho ho ho (laugh)

Move both of your index fingers up from the corners of your mouth.

4. love

With both of your hands in the "S" position, palms in, cross your wrists over your heart.

5. snow

With fingers spread and palms down, move your hands downward, and wiggle your fingers as they move.

6. sing

(Gesture) Place your closed fingertips at the corners of your mouth. Then move your hands forward and apart.

7. joy

Pat your chest with your open hands in an upward motion.

8. let

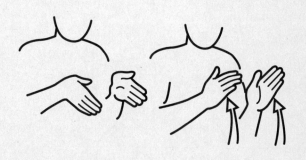

With palms facing each other and fingers pointing away from your body, move your hands in a scooping motion—down, then up.

Macmillan/McGraw-Hill

Name_____

9. ev'ryone

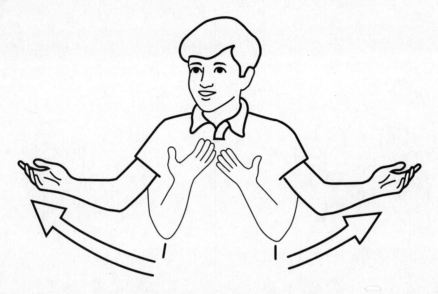

(Gesture) Hold your hands together, with palms up and fingers touching. Then move them apart in a sweeping gesture.

Macmillan/McGraw-Hill

Sing About Martin (Page 1)

1. sing

(Gesture) Place your closed fingertips at the corners of your mouth. Then move your hands forward and apart.

2. Martin (M)

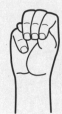

Sign the letter M *with your right hand for "Martin."*

3. caring

With both palms in, move your right hand back and forth between your chest and your left hand.

4. peace

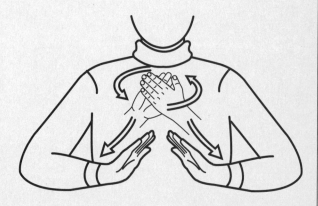

Place your right palm on your left palm. Turn the hands over. Then separate them, and move them down and sideways, palms down.

Grade 1 • Use with page T266.

Macmillan/McGraw-Hill

Sing About Martin (Page 2)

5. all around the world (all of us)

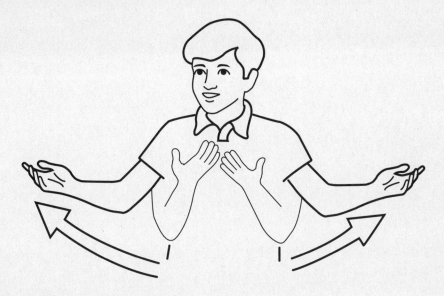

(Gesture) Hold your hands together, with palms up and fingers touching. Then move them apart in a sweeping gesture.

6. loving (love)

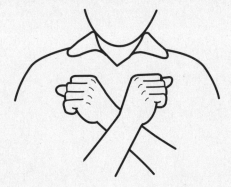

With both of your hands in the "S" position, palms in, cross your wrists over your heart.

GRADE 2

GRADE 2

1. here

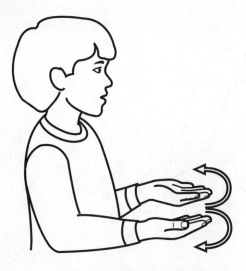

Hold both of your hands open, with palms up, and move them in small circles in opposite directions.

2. sit

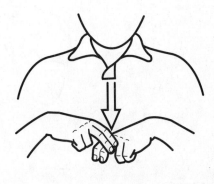

Bend both index and middle fingers slightly, palms down, and rest the right-hand fingers on the left-hand fingers.

3. ring (circle)

Point your right index finger out or down, and draw a circle in the air.

4. close your eyes

Place both hands, in the "Q" position, at your eyes. Close the index finger and thumb of each hand, and close your eyes until the word wide.

Macmillan/McGraw-Hill

5. hide

With your right hand in the "A" position, press the thumb to your lips. Then move the hand down and under your left hand, which is palm down. Hold this sign until the word wide.

6. wide

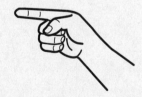

(Gesture) Open your eyes, and point to the empty space with your right index finger.

Macmillan/McGraw-Hill

Name _____

Who Has the Penny? (Page 1)

I. who

Make a circle in front of your mouth with your right index finger.

2. has/have

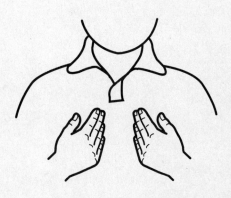

Touch your chest with the fingertips of your bent hands. Use the sign for both has *and* have.

3. penny

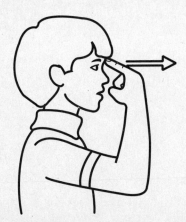

Touch your forehead with your right index finger. Then move the finger away.

4. I

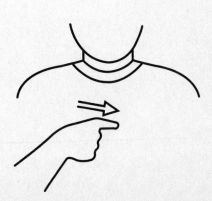

Point to your chest with your right index finger.

Who Has the Penny? (Page 2)

5. pin

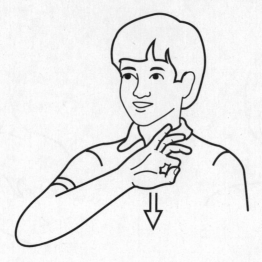

Make a circle with the thumb and index finger of your right hand, and touch the hand to your chest. Then move the hand down an inch. (This represents pinning on a brooch.)

Macmillan/McGraw-Hill

A Sailor Went to Sea, Sea, Sea

1. sea

Move your hands forward, making the motion of waves. (In sign language the meaning of the word is signed, not always the actual word. By using these signs, the song becomes much more understandable.)

2. see

Touch your right hand, in the "V" position, to beneath your right eye. Then move the hand forward.

Macmillan/McGraw-Hill

Take Me Out to the Ball Game (Page 1)

1. take me (bring)

Hold your hands open, with palms up, and move them from left to right. Then point to yourself on the word me.

2. ball game

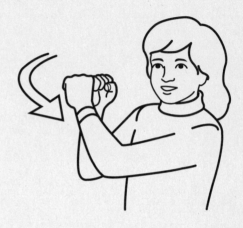

(Gesture) Make the natural motion of swinging a bat.

3. crowd

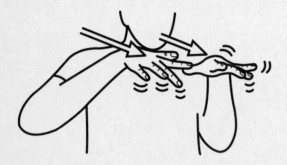

Hold your hands open, palms down, and move them forward while wiggling your fingers. (This shows the movement of many people.)

4. root (cheer)

With your right hand in the "X" position, wave an imaginary flag in small circles. (Both hands can be used for this sign.)

Name_____

Take Me Out to the Ball Game (Page 2)

5. shame

Touch your cheek with the back of the fingertips of your right hand. Then move the hand forward.

6. one

Hold up your right index finger.

7. two

Hold up the index finger and middle finger of your right hand.

8. three

Hold up the thumb, index finger, and middle finger of your right hand.

Macmillan/McGraw-Hill

Use with page 130. • Grade 2

9. **out**

(Gesture) Move your right hand, in the "A" position with thumb up, back across your shoulder. (This is the umpire's natural gesture for out.*)*

Frère Jacques (Are You Sleeping?) (Page 1)

I. are

Move your right hand, in the "R" position with palm facing left, from your lips forward.

2. you

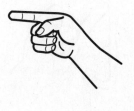

Point with your right index finger to the person you are talking to.

3. sleeping

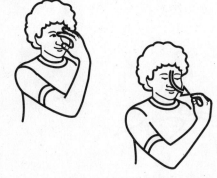

Touch your face with your open right hand. Then move the hand down while closing it. (This is to show the eyes closing.)

4. Brother

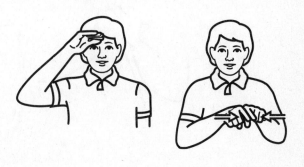

Open and close your right hand at your forehead. Then point your index fingers forward, palms down, and touch them together.

Frère Jacques (Are You Sleeping?) (Page 2)

5. John

Place your right hand, in the "J" position, over your heart. (You have given John a "name sign," rather than having to fingerspell his name.)

6. morning

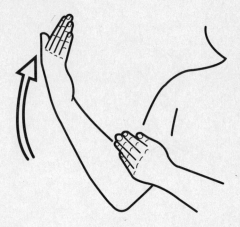

Place the fingertips of your left hand in the bend of your right arm. Then move your open right palm upward toward your body.

7. bells

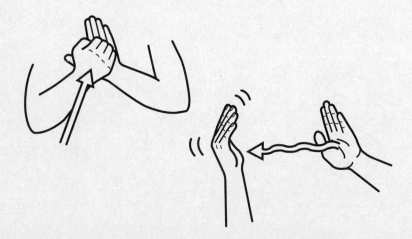

Hit the open palm of your left hand with your right fist. Then move your right hand out, opening and shaking it as it moves. Repeat the sign four more times for <u>ding</u>, ding, <u>dong</u>, <u>ding</u>, ding, <u>dong</u>.

Name_____

Who's That Tapping at the Window? (Page 1)

1. who's

Make a circle in front of your mouth with your right index finger.

2. that

Place your right hand, in the "Y" position with palm out, on an imaginary window in front of you.

3. tapping/knocking

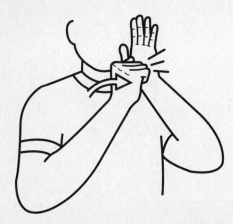

Hit your left palm with the knuckles of your right hand two times for tapping at the *and two times for* knocking at the.

4. window

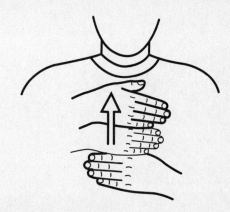

Hold your open left hand pointing right. Place your open right hand, pointing left, on the edge of the left hand. Then move the right hand up a few inches.

Who's That Tapping at the Window? (Page 2)

5. door

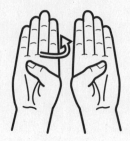

Hold both hands in the "B" position, with palms facing out and index fingers touching. Then swing the right hand back and forth to show a door opening and closing.

6. I

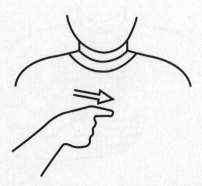

Point to your chest with your right index finger.

7. am

Touch your lips with the tip of your right index finger. Then move the hand straight ahead.

Macmillan/McGraw-Hill

Name _____

1. my

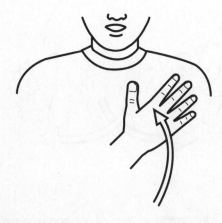

Touch your chest with your open right hand.

2. country/land

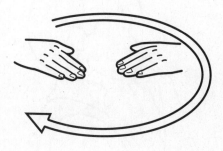

(Gesture) With both palms down and hands open, make a large circle with your right hand over your left hand.

3. 'tis (is)

Touch your lips with the tip of your right index finger. Then move the hand straight ahead.

4. of thee

(Gesture) Hold your hands together, with palms up and fingers touching. Then move them apart in a sweeping gesture.

5. sweet

Move the fingertips of your right hand down across your chin.

6. liberty

Cross your hands, in the "L" position with palms in, at the wrists. Then uncross them, move them apart, and turn palms out.

7. sing

(Gesture) Place your closed fingertips at the corners of your mouth. Then move your hands forward and apart.

8. where

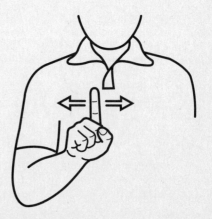

Hold up your right index finger, with the palm of the hand out, and move it back and forth.

9. fathers (ancestors)

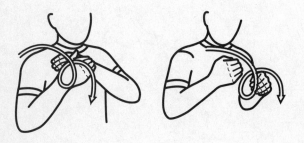

Roll your hands forward from your right shoulder.

10. died

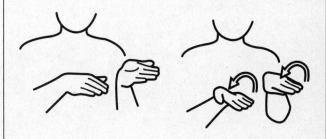

Point the fingers of both hands straight ahead, with the right palm down and the left palm up. Then turn both hands over.

11. Pilgrim's

With both hands in the "P" position, touch them together above your head. Move them apart and then down to outline a Pilgrim's hat.

12. pride

With your right hand in the "A" position, move the thumb up your chest.

Macmillan/McGraw-Hill

13. from

Point your left index finger up. Touch your right hand, in the "X" position, to the left index finger. Then move the right hand away.

14. ev'ry

With both hands in the "A" position, draw your right thumb down your left thumb several times.

15. mountainside

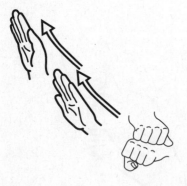

Strike your fists together, palms down and right fist above the left. Then raise your open hands toward your right side.

16. let

With palms facing each other and fingers pointing away from your body, move your hands in a scooping motion—down, then up.

17. freedom

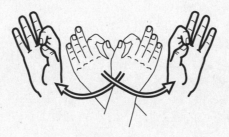

Cross your hands, in the "F" position with palms in, at the wrists. Then uncross them, move them apart, and turn palms out.

18. ring

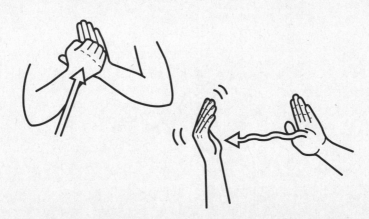

Hit the open palm of your left hand with your right fist. Then move your right hand out, opening and shaking it as it moves.

Name_____

The Thing That Isn't There

I. thing

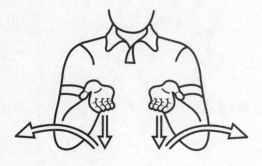

Hold your hands open, with palms up, and move them down and apart.

2. isn't (not)

Cross your open hands, with palms down. Then move the hands apart (like "safe" in baseball).

3. there

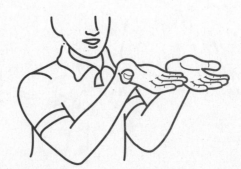

Turn both of your palms up after the word isn't.

Name_____

I. he

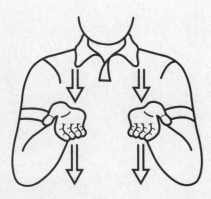

Gesture to an imaginary person, from head to toe, with both of your hands, palms up.

2. wanted

Hold both of your hands open, with palms up. Then bend the fingers and move them toward your body.

3. peace

Place your right palm on your left palm. Turn the hands over. Then separate them, and move them down and sideways, palms down.

4. love/loving

With both of your hands in the "S" position, palms in, cross your wrists over your heart.

Macmillan/McGraw-Hill

Martin Luther King (Page 2)

5. land

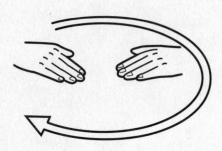

(Gesture) With both palms down and hands open, make a large circle with your right hand over your left hand.

6. Martin (M)

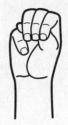

Sign the letter M with your right hand for "Martin."

7. Luther (L)

Sign the letter L with your right hand for "Luther."

8. King

Hold your right hand in the "K" position at your left shoulder. Then move the hand to the right side of your waist as if drawing a king's sash.

Martin Luther King (Page 3)

---

9. man

Grasp the brim of an imaginary baseball hat with your right hand. Then move the hand down and into the "5" position, and touch your chest with the thumb.

You Are My Sunshine (Page 1)

1. you

Point with your right index finger to the person you are talking to.

2. are (be)

Touch your lips with the tip of your right index finger. Then move the hand straight ahead.

3. sunshine

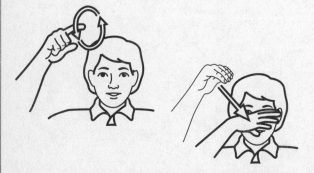

Circle your right index finger above your head. Then close the fingertips, and move the hand down while opening it.

4. only

Hold your right index finger upright, with palm out. Then, with an upward swing, turn the hand to palm in.

Macmillan/McGraw-Hill

You Are My Sunshine (Page 2)

5. make

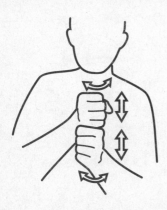

With both hands in the "S" position, place your right hand on top of your left. Twist the two fists and strike them together.

6. happy

Pat your chest with your open hands in an upward motion.

7. when (happen)

Point both index fingers away from your body, with palms facing. Then turn your hands so the palms are facing down.

8. skies

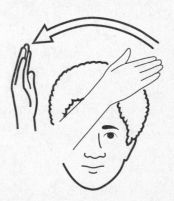

Make a large arc above your head with your right hand.

Macmillan/McGraw-Hill

9. gray (dark)

Cross your hands in front of your face, palms in, as if closing out the light.

10. never

Make a question mark in the air with your right hand, held upright with fingers together.

11. know

Touch your forehead with the fingertips of your right hand.

12. Dear (sweet)

Move the fingertips of your right hand down across your chin.

Grade 2 • Use with page 285.

Name_____

13. how much

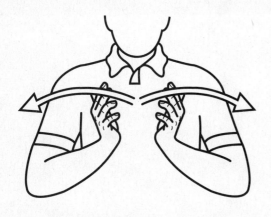

Hold both hands upright, with palms facing each other and fingers open. Move the hands apart as if describing an amount.

14. love

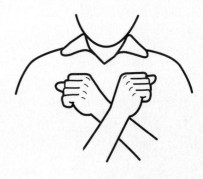

With both of your hands in the "S" position, palms in, cross your wrists over your heart.

15. don't

Cross your open hands, with palms down. Then move the hands apart (like "safe" in baseball).

16. away (erase)

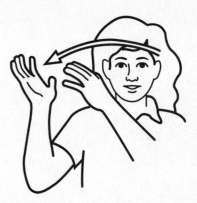

Make a sweeping gesture in the air with both hands.

Macmillan/McGraw-Hill